The Immortal You

Death is Defeated

Luke Agee

Contents

Preface

There are many reasons to believe that we all must die. We hear it all of our lives that we are guaranteed death as our "end". I understand completely why so many think that and are fully convinced by that. We see death every day and have experienced it with loved ones and close friends. We have grown accustomed to it and have accepted it as part of the gospel. That we have death to look forward to as a gate into the glorious heaven that Jesus paid the price for us to enter into has become a major cornerstone of the christian belief for many generations.

Yet what if there is another reality? What if we have missed a huge part of the gospel truth that Jesus was showing and bringing to us? Why do we readily run with a message that presents us with a facing of death that scripture tells us was defeated by Jesus and His glorious resurrection?

Jesus is the Way. The Way into what? Wow. So many things that are too numerous to cover in this one book. The one thing we will focus on as you can tell so far is the way He made for us into Life. For He is Life. John 1:4 says that Jesus is the Life that is the Light of men. Jesus is Life and therefore there is no death in Him. We now have Him in us and we are now in Him. Thus we are in Life and Life is in us. Which also means that our bond with death is disconnected and ended in Christ who is our life.

In this book we are going to cover the mystery Jesus taught us as well as others in the scriptures about immortal life that now belongs to us. I know that this is a heavy topic and for many an unheard of reality. We must remember though that unless we are shown or taught anything we cannot have the ability to believe in it. As the apostle Paul tells us, faith comes by hearing. If no one hears they cannot have faith.

So my hope for you in reading this book is to not only unveil this powerful truth but also to awaken faith within you about never having to die. To be able to have faith that you are now no longer susceptible to death and can truly live forever without having to ever taste of death because of what Jesus has done for you.

Chapter 1

There are many scriptures that have become a staple of the church teachings for heaven and hell theology that don't even mention either of those dimensions in the very scriptures used. What they do mention though are either life, death or both in those verses. When we revisit these scriptures based on what they are actually saying it will give you a fresh perspective of what is meant to be conveyed.

The first one we will look at is probably the most famous scripture ever, John 3:16. John 3:16 says "For God so loved the world that He gave His only begotten Son, that whosoever believes in Him should NOT PERISH but have EVERLASTING LIFE. So as we look at this again we see that the issue being addressed is perishing, or dying. The solution being offered is whoever believes shall be able to have everlasting, or immortal, life.

There is nothing mentioned at all here about heaven or hell. There is nothing mentioned here about repentance or sins. What is mentioned here is the ability to have a cure for perishing through the means of believing in the begotten Son. Belief in all that He has accomplished and in who He says He is, has become a gate or way into life. Permanent, lasting, and immortal life.

There is nothing here that says that you will have to die first then enter into immortality. For some reason though this is how this scripture has been seen and taught for the most part. So many agree that we will live forever and eternally, yet only after we lay our physical bodies down by perishing. Why? This scripture does not say that. In fact it says quite the opposite. Only because we have been taught it the way of death it now seems as if that is the truth of the verse. As well as because we think that everyone must die because it is what we have seen our whole lives. This is why we must renew our minds from the false mindsets to the new mindsets of the mind of Christ we now have.

Another one we will take a look at now is Romans 6:23. This verse is used so strongly by those who desire others to see our Father as a tyrant yelling at them about their sins. Well there is much more to this verse and it is actually quite powerful and encouraging when seen the right way.

Romans 6:23 states "For the wages of sin is death, but the gift of God is ETERNAL LIFE in Christ Jesus our Lord." (I am taking the position of assuming that you already know that Jesus bore all sin and removed it fully from us as a foundation before acknowledging the rest.) Once again what we don't see here is heaven or hell mentioned. What we do see mentioned again though is death and life. Death that is the wage to pay for sins. Life that is a gift from our Father since Jesus has now removed our sins. The word used here for Eternal is the greek word 'aionios', which means 'without end', 'never to cease', and "forever".

The word for life used is "zoe" which literally means "life". So when we put that phrase together it means life without end or life without ceasing. Hallelujah what an awesome gift that has been given to us! A gift is something freely handed to you without you ever having to try to work for it or earn it. Life without ceasing or ending is now a free gift given to you by the Father through Jesus Christ! Nowhere does that include having to die in any way, shape, or form. Life eternal is freely given to you with only the stipulation of believing it was given to you in the Son so as to arc with life to make it a reality.

Now only two scriptures in and I am sure you are now scratching your head curious if this could possibly be true and asking yourself why you have never been told this before. Or you may be ready to toss it all out and stop reading this book. While that is absolutely your choice and you are empowered to disagree with me, I ask of you to stick with me for some more insight on this topic and evidence to point to it overwhelmingly.

Another amazing scripture along these lines is Romans 8:2 which says "For the law of the Spirit of LIFE in Christ Jesus has set me free from the law of sin and DEATH." The law that showed forth sin was bringing death and Jesus brought a new and living law by governance of the Spirit that was Life. Death was ended as the law was fulfilled in Christ and being overtaken by a new means of law from the Spirit that carried in it the completeness of Life without end!

See the pattern that is forming here? Death has always been a major issue and unintentional by the Father.

Death as we all know came from Adam and the choice that was made to eat of the wrong tree. Death became a starving force that consumed almost all without prejudice since the day that it was introduced into the earth. This was until Jesus came with the Spirit of the Father and a law of Life that is written in the Sprits DNA. He released that Life unto us by His blood and Spirit and took us into a new realm of freedom from death.

While the overwhelming majority suggest that Isaiah 25:8 is for sometime after an end of the world or an apocalypse, I submit to you that it is actually speaking of the time when Jesus comes to reveal He is the Life and will defeat death with His resurrection. Isaiah 25:8 says "He (Jesus) will swallow up death forever." I believe we can all agree that with Jesus' resurrection He defeated death and it is a forever victory. The only thing we have a hang up with is that applying to us. I get it.

Although we must understand that it is the same faith that leads us to salvation knowledge that also opens the door to the more of what Jesus accomplished for us. This includes swallowing up death for us in His

Life. He removed the shadow of death that had been cast all over the human race with the glorious and brilliant Light of eternal and immortal Life that is the very essence of our Father God.

Now that we have covered these scriptures again through the lens of the completed work of the cross of Christ I hope that there is that fire within you burning in resonation of the truth of life. Alive in Christ means so much more than we have been told but this is a generation coming awake to the fullness. Hallelujah!

Chapter 2

Jesus says one of the most powerful and profound things in John 11. I also feel it is one of the most over-looked things said as well. In John 11:25 Jesus says "I am the resurrection and the life. He who believes in Me, though he may die, he shall live." Come on! That's so awesome and amazing. He is the resurrection He says. Not that He is going to just be the only one to resurrect or that it will be a future event in time, but that resurrection is synonymous with Him! That when you see Him you see the resurrection. Just think and meditate on that for a moment.

Resurrection is not something separate from Jesus. It is not an event or an action of another spirit from the Lord. Resurrection is the person of Jesus Christ! This means that us being in Him is being in the resurrec-tion. There is no death in resurrection. There is only Life. There is only the power of Jesus that swallows up death.

Also we glean from this sentence that in Christ a per-son can have a bodily death and still live because they are in Christ who is the resurrection. This is a major staple in the Christian faith of course. We are eternal and spirit and not flesh alone so therefore the passing of the flesh is nowhere near the end of us. This is such an amazing and encouraging thing that could be all and be enough. It is not the only option though.

He says an even more profound thing in the next verse. A statement that has confounded and stumped many theologians for generations and thousands of years. A deep revelatory statement that is the crux of what has the ability to change our minds and lives eternally.

John 11:26 says "And whoever lives and believes in me shall NEVER DIE. Do you believe this?" Now that is huge. There is so much here being said that is absolutely mind blowing. Jesus is literally telling us that someone can be alive in the flesh, believe in Jesus and what He has done, and then due to that never die. Never die. I really hope that this is sinking in and hitting a nerve. Even if it is offending your mind let it be caught instead in your spirit. You will see that it is going to ring true with your spirit man and you won't be able to let it go without seeking more on it. Then you will find that the Bible is actually packed full of evidence of this actuality.

Jesus raising Lazarus from the dead was even Him making a statement to the people of that day that He had complete control over death. He never even wanted to call Lazarus dead when His disciples were asking Him what was going on with him. He always called it being asleep. Same thing when Jesus raised a little girl from the dead. He also then referenced it as being asleep. Jesus wouldn't even acknowledge death having any place at all amongst Him.

The way Jesus showed that He had complete authority over death was not only just in raising Lazarus from the dead but also in how He did. The Jewish people have and had a belief that when someone dies that their soul stays with them for three days before moving on to another realm and therefore causing the body of that person to perish permanently without hope of returning to their body .

This is the reason why Jesus waited specifically three days before arriving to the tomb of Lazarus. Showing up on the fourth day caused many who had any hope of Jesus doing something to save and help Lazarus to doubt and lose faith that He could now. Yet Jesus did this to prove not only could He have prevented Lazarus from dying, but He could also raise him from the dead with no limitation at all on how or when He could. He revealed to all there at the tomb that He had absolute authority over death.

When He spoke for Lazarus to come forth, I believe that He had to say the name of Lazarus specifically or else all the people in all the tombs would have come out resurrected. This is the true power and dominion of the One who says I AM the Resurrection and the LIFE.

Chapter 3

"Most assuredly I say to you, whoever believes in Me has everlasting life." John 6:47. This is not that hard of a task for us when you think about it. We need only to believe in Jesus to have everlasting life. I do want to point out once again that there is no mention of having to die first then have life. For some reason that is all I have ever been taught though. I am willing to bet that this is what you have been told also or have assumed from all we have seen in life. That we believe in Jesus then have to pass away then we get to go to heaven, and that this is the gospel of everlasting life. No it is so much more!

He continues on to say in verses 48-51 "I am the Bread of Life. Your fathers ate the bread in the wilderness, and are dead. This is the bread which comes down from heaven, that one may eat of it and NOT DIE. I am the living bread which came down from heaven. If anyone eats of this bread, he will LIVE FOREVER; and the bread that I shall give is My flesh, which I shall give for the life of the world."

This is Jesus literally telling us the exact opposite of the line of thought that says we must die then live by going to heaven to have everlasting life. No. See it is not that because Jesus is saying that His flesh is being given so that we can live forever and not die. Parabolically what He is saying is that His death is also our death and that His physical body is being given as the place of our physical body. We must understand that we were in Him on the cross and that His death is and was our death. Our death and funeral was in the past! We have already died!

Paul knew this when he said in Galatians 2:20 that he had been crucified with Christ. So have you and I.

2 Corinthians 5:14 says that "One died for all therefore all died." There is truly no other death needed for us to experience when we can just know this and then believe in it. I can feel you thinking about how Paul still died. Well we will get more into that in another chapter. Paul was actually immortal and proved it in his life. I will go deeper on that soon.

Jesus was painting a powerful picture for those listening to Him when He spoke in John 6. He knew how important and treasured the story of the Israelites being taken through and being fed in the wilderness was to the Jews there. He wanted them to see that the wilderness encounter with manna was just a shadow and picture of the true Manna coming in the future for the people of Israel and for the world. That in the shadow of the real there was death that still had a part and place in it. In the real though that was not the shadow, in Jesus, death was no more a part and had no place.

He is the living Bread. That means alive and full of Life. That although the fathers could eat the daily manna in the wilderness and still die, this was a new bread that had not been eaten by them. This was brand new and not capable of allowing any one to die when it is truly eaten. This Bread, the flesh of Jesus, can never spoil or rot. His flesh is eternally Life for all who desire to feast on Him. This is the Bread of Life that is feasted on eternally as the food of Heaven.

The Israelites received fresh manna daily as a picture of being fed from above with the Bread of Life. Yet it was fresh only on a daily basis and for two days only for the sake of the Sabbath. This is a deep metaphor within itself of the fresh daily bread the Lord told the disciples to pray for daily. Yet most importantly it shows that it still could rot and spoil since it was only meant for one day. Therefore, the flesh and Bread of Christ is on a higher divine truth since it can never become ruined or rotted. It is meant for everyday and the infinite Today that is Christ.

He had already told us a divine mystery when He spoke to satan in Matthew 4 and said that "Man does not live by bread alone but by every word that proceeds from out of the mouth of God." The fathers in the wilderness had eaten of bread alone. They had not engaged in faith enough to be able to move on past the natural bread and manna into the spiritual. This is why Hebrews 4 tells us that the gospel was preached to them but that the word that they heard (and saw in their life lived out I will add) did not profit them, not being mixed with faith in those who heard it.

See they were living out a picture and parable of the gospel by their very existence and life. They were pointing to the Messiah and Him being the bread of Life while not receiving it as such and therefore died in the parable. I hope that made sense to you. That is a powerful nugget when you catch it. Jesus though showed up in a new time frame and manifested the true Bread of Life that He is, has always been and forever will be eternally.

Seeing Him as He is and what He has done in His sacrifice mixed with the faith to feast on it daily creates within us life. This is why we must feast on His flesh. We must feast on His and our death, burial, resurrection, and ascension to the Father. We must drink of His blood, poured out for us to remove all DNA impurities out of our bloodline, so that we might have everlasting life. It is a renewing of our mind that brings transformation. Renewing our minds from death to life by meditating and feasting upon the sacrifice of Jesus body and digesting in our hearts and minds the blood of the Lamb being shed for the world.

Chapter 4

Death has become such a readily accepted thought process amongst those who believe in Jesus because the church has grabbed ahold of death as a type of door or gateway into heaven. This is the lowest capacity for entering into heaven though. It is still from the grace of the Father that it is an option. Basically in an almost harsh sounding way to put it, it is still there due to immaturity of the knowledge of believers. It is like a safety net or backup plan for anyone who cannot grasp the reality of immortality.

We see the pattern of the Lord and Enoch and others as a powerful truth for them and then look at all that have died and have a choice to make. We can look at the truth of life for us and as a reality we can have or we can look at all of the death and agree with it. This is a daily choice for every choice we make honestly. This is why the Lord spoke to the Israelites in the Old Testament and gave them that same choice.

Deuteronomy 30:19-20 AMP says "I call heaven and earth to witness against you today, that I have set before you LIFE AND DEATH, blessing and curse. Therefore choose LIFE, that you and your offspring may LIVE, loving the Lord your God, obeying His voice and holding fast to Him, for He is your LIFE (YOUR GOOD LIFE, YOUR ABUNDANT LIFE, YOUR FULFILLMENT) AND LENGTH OF DAYS."

See it is nothing new from the heart of the Father to give the people of the earth the ability to choose to have abundant life and live from His word and energy of His breath. It wasn't just so that they could have the ability to live just for that day or for a few days. It was so that they could truly live forever and eternally. That is why He said life and length of days. This is why Jesus brought that same message and a better way into that reality. Through His death and flesh of Life!

Also it wasn't just for you. He says in the verse in Deuteronomy we just looked at that He wanted it for us and our offspring. He has always wanted it to be the knowledge that we shared and taught to our off-spring so that they would have it as truth hidden in their hearts and dominate in the thoughts of their minds.

The love of the Father is to have all with Him and to see all have the desire of His heart. Which is life and it abundant, immortal, everlasting, and eternal. This is why Peter says in 2 Peter 3:9 that the Lord wishes none should perish. Not perishing means not dying. That your body would not die or ever see decay but experience the swallowing up of Life. Life swallowing up your body!

You are already eternal as a spirit being. So of course that is not the question or resistance many have about eternal life. It is all about the question of our body being able to be immortal and eternal. Enoch shows us this is a reality. Elijah showed us this is a reality. Adam was supposed to show us this reality. Jesus showed us this is a reality. Paul showed us this is a reality. Many many others also who are not as famous or well known showed us this too.

So how did death become such a powerful narrative and the mindset humanity took towards heaven and relationship with the Lord Almighty? Lets dive into that in this next chapter.

Chapter 5

Death is a grace from the Lord that was only meant for a season and to become overcome by coming up higher to the original place of life that we were blue-printed with. Death is still a grace for those who are not taught or shown the greater truth of Life eternal and immortal in Christ. It was never the genesis or permanent intention of the Most High for access to Him or to our homeland of heavenly places.

1 Corinthians 15:21 tells us that by man came death into the world. This does not tell us that specifically this man was Adam, although the large large majority tells us that he is the one who brought death into the world. I am not so convinced but that is not the focus of this book. Either way death came by a man and exists because of man.

The grace part of it comes from Genesis 3 and how the Lord responded to the specific actions of Adam and Eve. Genesis 3:22-23 says "Then the Lord God said, Bchold, the man has become like one of us in knowing good and evil. Now, lest he reach out his hand and take also of the tree of life and eat, and live forever-, therefore the Lord God sent him out from the garden of Eden to work the ground from which he was taken."

Breaking this down we see that the ability to eat from the tree of life in a state of fallen or sinful nature was so troubling to the Lord that He didn't even want to finish His statement about what would happen if they could eat from the tree of life in that state. It was such a horrific thought to the Lord and something that He didn't even want to speak out loud about.

I believe that this is due to Adam and Eve being meant to be eternal by eating from the tree of life and if they were able to continue to do so that they would stay eternal but eternal in a fallen lesser state of sinful nature and perpetual decay and darkness without ever being able to be freed from it. Think about this for a moment and grasp the horror the Lord felt with this.

Mankind would be able to stay eternal and immortal but it would be in a place of conditions of death without being able to die. They would have children and if that child was born deformed, sick, blind, deaf, or paralyzed due to sin and death existing in man now there would be never any end to that state. That child would be eternally that nature. If an adult caught a terrible disease or infection or cancer they would have no end to that ever. My goodness thats such a devastating and heartbreaking thought.

That was why the Lord couldn't even bear to think about it either or to even speak out that wicked possibility. It was such a detrimental reality that could take place that the Lord decided at the moment that He would have to give a grace. To give a means of being able to see an end to that horrid scenario by way of that person not staying trapped in a body that was eternally riddled with any type of deathly nature.

Therefore He removed from them the ability to eat of the tree of life by removing them from the garden of Eden and reengaged man with the ability to have death by placing them back into an environment where there would have to toil and labor from the curse of sin and thus death. Thus, death became a door to ending suffering amongst man because of the love of the Lord for humanity. This was not intended to be the greatest truth or access point for man to engage with health and wholeness and life though still.

This is why Enoch did not taste death as we know it. This was why Elijah did not taste death as we know it. This is why Moses did not taste death as we know it. This is why the elders who went up the mountain with Moses to see the Lord did not taste death as we know it. For in Exodus 24 the elders went up on the mountain in the presence of Yahweh and they never came back down. They ascended into the cloud and stayed there without tasting death.

There have been many who have tasted and seen that the Lord has had a desire for man to return to eating from the tree of life by means of Christ no matter where they were in the timeline.

The cross is an everlasting truth that supersedes time and can be engaged with at any point of the timeline of eternity and these men knew this. Man can take their body into a realm of life and glory and immortality through the presence of the Lord where there is no death or decay and they were aware of this. Many have been able to take themselves through the flaming sword of the Lord that was placed outside the entrance of the garden of Eden, not to keep out, mind you, but to guide THE WAY TO the tree of life, and then eat of the Bread of resurrection Life which is the flesh of Jesus.

This is still the accessibility we have now and will always have forevermore. The same Door and same Way as always. The Way and Door of the flesh of Jesus.

If we do not know this though or do not see it or have it taught to us then we take on the mindset of death being agreeable and necessary. Faith comes by hearing and if we have never been taught that the Lord truly eliminated the door of death and eliminated the need of it and that death is a necessity and just a part of life then we perpetuate it and allow it to continue because our faith is in that perception.

This is the reason why the grace of death has become the avenue in which mainstream has said is the access point of eternal life and heaven and an escape from the corruption of this world and our bodies. Yet, when we know the truth of the fullness of what Christ has done on the cross and for all of creation we realize that death is not only defeated but also all of the things that try to attack the mind and the body. Sin, sickness, disease, decay, and death has all been defeated and therefore the body is not to be subjected to any of it when we engage that truth and apply it to our focus and heart.

We must cut our ties with a futuristic death and shift our mindset to the mind of Christ in which is the knowledge that our death was in the past and is eternally removed and over. We don't need to plan on a funeral or a time in which we will have to die and pass on. We need to be planning for the years ahead that we are going to continue to live in and our family is going to continue to live in to bring the Kingdom to the earth! Our bond and connection to death is dead and buried! The necessity of death as a grace to be free from suffering is over and gone!

We were co-crucified, co-buried, co-resurrected, and we co-ascended with and in Christ Jesus our Lord! None of those things need to or must ever happen again. It is finished in the one who is the Beginning and the End!

Chapter 6

Jesus said that His life could not be take from Him but that only if He laid it down could He taste death. This is the same truth we must wrap our heads and hearts around. This is the same exact reality for all of us in Christ. We so easily see that for Jesus and say oh of course and agree. Although, when we think about it for ourselves we either have no grid for it or just a small grid that is trying to maintain that thought process while fighting against what is visible every-day, which is death and decay. This is why why we must shift our eyes from the realm of death in this third dimensional realm into the realm of Life that is in Christ Jesus.

Romans 8:2 tells us that we have been set free from the law of sin and death by the law of the Spirt of Life in Christ. We no longer have a law of death to engage with or entangle with or be bound to. Sin and death both are now eternally removed from our nature and dna. That is now in your physical body! Not one day over yonder or one day without your body. It is a present truth with all the aspects of your being. Especially including your physical body never dying because there is no more law for it ever again.

So much of what we expect or can believe to be real in the future is absolutely what we need to grab ahold of now for ourselves and our family. Everything that we need for life and godliness has been given to us fully now in the person of Christ. Who is who we live and move in. We no longer are alive within our own selves or own existence. We are now alive within the Son of God and it is no longer us that live but Him through us. He can never taste death ever again by His choice and that is the same answer for us now!

We don't even need to try to figure out how to eat from the tree of life in the garden of Eden anymore either. We just need to fasten our gaze and our diet upon the flesh and Body of Christ in which is eternal Life. This very flesh and Body that we are now intertwined with as one with for all of the rest of our existence.

1 Corinthians 6:17 tells us that he who is joined to the Lord is now one Spirit with Him. Taking it a step fur-

ther, we all know that we are one Body with Him. Ephesians 4:4 says that there is one Body and one Spirit. This is the Body and Spirit of the Lord that we are now permanently fused and grafted into. Galatians 3:27 says that if you were baptized into Christ you have put on Christ. A literal form of this scripture is that when you are baptized into Christ you have become Christ!

This is from the understanding that you are no longer your own and have laid down your life in the baptism into the death and burial of Christ and have now taken on His very life in your body and have taken His Spirit as your own. That you no longer are the one who lives but it is Christ within you that lives. That He in us and as us is still manifesting and releasing the Kingdom and the will of the Father. Including complete victory over and freedom from death.

What this all means is that we have to get ahold of the reality that when Jesus said that His life could not be taken from Him, it applies to us as well. We have to decide that this is the same reality for us also. We cannot have our lives taken from us but only if we lay them down can they end in the flesh. Otherwise we are to stay alive in the body and become transfigured as Jesus did and become fully light forever.

We have to catch onto the fact that what was and is the applicable scenario to Jesus is the same for us everyday from now on since the moment we were born from above. It is about needing to have our minds renewed to the Truth of Christ and our existence in Him and as Him in the earth. Maybe in another book one day will we engage with transfiguration and this awesome part of the Gospel usually overlooked or not known.

Someone who did understand that he was immortal and not able to have his life taken from him was Paul. His life was attacked and death was thrust on him numerous times and he walked away alive from it all. As a matter of my opinion and many other scholars opinions, he was actually killed and resurrected a few times in his life.

In Acts 28:3-6 it says "When Paul had gathered a bundle of sticks and put them on the fire, a viper came out because of the heat and fastened on his hand. When the native people saw the creature hanging from his hand, they said to one another, "no doubt this man is a murderer. Though he has escaped from the sea, Justice has not allowed him to live." Paul, however, shook off the creature into the fire and suffered no harm. They were waiting for him to swell up or suddenly fall down dead. But when they had waited a long time and saw no misfortune come to him, they changed their minds and said that he was a god.

Paul literally had venom go into his veins from a snake bite and did not have any negative side effects at all from it. He embodied and manifested the words spoken by Jesus that even if we would drink or ingest poison it could not harm us. Can snake venom harm Jesus? Absolutely not! So Paul also knew that it could not harm him. He knew that the blood of Jesus in his veins would destroy the vile venom. Thus it did. We must also know and understand that venom or poison of any kind would die if the blood of Jesus in our veins ever came in contact with it. Same goes for any sickness or disease or affliction also!

In 2 Corinthians 11: 24-27 Paul describes many brutal things that he endured in life. Including being beaten with rods, shipwrecked in the ocean, being stoned, sleep exhaustion, as well as starvation and dehydration. Yet none of this could kill him or steal life from his mortal body. He knew the Christ life within that he was one with would swallow up those afflictions and sustain him in any way needed.

In Acts 14:19-20 is one of my favorite and mind blowing stories in the bible. Especially when we break down and explore what truly took place. It says "but jews came from Antioch and Iconia, and having persuaded the crowds, they stoned Paul and dragged him out of the city, supposing him dead. But when the disciples gathered about him, he rose up and entered the city, and on the next day he went on with Barnabas to Derbe."

What??! He was stoned to death (many scholars believe he was actually left for dead as dead due to how the Jews would stone for the purpose of punishment by death and not to just harm) and then it says that he just got up and went back into the city! Come on now! So whether he just resurrected or entered into a realm of glory and then picked his body back up I am not sure but the point is the same. He was not going to be ended that day by anyone or anything. Paul knew he had more to do and accomplish and death was not going to stop him from that and that it could not take him.

A man that has just been stoned with large rocks and left for dead does not just get up and walk under his own power back into the city or make a trip by foot the very next day to another city miles away. This only comes to pass from a supernatural manifestation taking place.

Which was the fact that the life of Christ had swallowed up Pauls body and he was submitted to that life having complete control. Thereby death from a thief wanting to take his life by means of stoning was not possible. Hallelujah!

Paul was immortal and eternal same as Christ. He lived it and walked it out daily. I always still get asked though, well Paul died so how do you explain that? Easily and I have in what I have already written. When and how he died was by choice alone. Nothing could take his life just as Jesus had said and proved. Although, when Paul decided it was time to leave behind his physical body he said that he had run his course and finished his race and was ready to choose to die by laying his life down. This is and was the only reason why.

In Philippians 1:21-24 is a powerful example of Paul showing his mindset on being eternal and immortal and making a conscious choice about whether to stay in his body for more time or choosing to pass on to a different realm of eternity. He says here "For me to live is Christ, and for me to die is gain. If I am in the flesh, that means fruitful labor for me. Yet which I shall choose I cannot tell. I am hard pressed between the two. My desire is to depart and be with Christ, for that is far better. But to remain in the flesh is more necessary on your account."

Paul actually just explained to us in these verses written to the Philippians that he had the ability to choose to die or not. He knew that he had authority over death in Christ and could prolong it, never choose it, or accept it at any time. This is part of the gospel and fully real and true in the finished work of Christ!

Just like as when Jesus was in the garden of Gethsemane and had the choice to not taste or experience death at all he chose to do it. It was possible without a doubt that He could have decided not to and we would not have the same scenario in the world and in life as we do now. Not even close. Thankfully though this is not the case and Jesus decided to take on the will of the Father and taste death for all mankind by His choice alone. His choice to agree with the Father and have all of the world be brought into His death and then consequently His life. This is the gospel. This is the glad tidings of good news that Paul and the disciples knew about.

Chapter 7

Someone else who did not taste death in the traditional way to me and many other scholars is Moses. Now there are certainly a large number of people who believe that he definitely did taste death. That's fine and they are empowered to believe so. I just want to submit to you the possibility that maybe he didn't. Lets look at the evidence.

Moses spends a grand total of 80 days in mans time on the mountain and in the cloud of glory with Yahweh. When he comes back down he is now totally glowing and shining with the radiance of the Life and glory of the presence and face of the Lord. Moses has become a living light being that looks just as like Him who is Light. Jesus the Christ and Lord Almighty.

Moses, I believe, was actually taken up into the cloud by the Lord and then transported through time and space to the place known as the mount of transfiguration mentioned in Mark 9. This is of course where Jesus becomes transfigured as Light and appears to the disciples as such and is accompanied by Moses and

Elijah. So since Moses had asked of the Lord one thing, which was to see the glory of the Lord, he was answered with being allowed to see the face of the transfigured Christ on that mountain in a time frame that man would call the future. Then Moses is taken back to the time frame in which man would call present where he ascended the mountain.

Therefore when he comes back down the mountain he is appearing just as like that same glorious nature of the Lord that he took on by being there in that glory realm of Jesus' radiant presence. Or in other words he is no longer a normal human but now a person swallowed up and clothed in the glory of the Lord. His body is now saturated and overflowing with the Life of the Lord that cannot have death anywhere inside it unintentionally.

This is why it says of Moses later when he is supposed to have died that his legs had not grown weak and his eyes had not grown dim. That he was still so filled with life that he was like a young man. Deuteronomy says that Moses was 120 years old and his vigor unabated and eyes never dimmed. Yet that he died according to the word of the Lord and his body buried by the Lord somewhere his body was never found.

To me this is because he wasn't taken through a death that we think of when we think of dying. Think of it as a transition from in his body to outside of his body without his body actually losing life and breath. That it was a transition and a preservation of his body with his breath in it for a future date to come. Similar to what I feel took place with Enoch. That Moses and Enoch were as a certain way and then were now of a different state and form outside of their natural body without losing their bodies permanently at all. We all are to keep our bodies eternally.

I know that this is hard to see for some and maybe it is not what happened at all. This is just a suggestion to meditate on and ponder. I could obviously write quite a bit more about the scenario with Enoch and even with Elijah but so much has been spoken and taught about their skipping death that I don't feel I need to touch on them as much.

Another follower of Christ who knew that his death was fulfilled in Jesus and that he had no other death that he needed to partake of was the disciple named John the beloved. He is the one spoken of in John 21 by Jesus when He said "If it is My will that he remain until I come, what is that to you?" Because of Jesus saying this many who heard that it was said believed that Jesus was saying that John would never die. Now that is up for debate still among biblical scholars but I am not so sure that he ever did die. This is why.

John was put on the Island of Patmos for a very amazing and astounding reason. The governmental leadership of his day had tried to kill him many different ways. Like Paul, he never did die from any of these attempts. He survived and overcame being dragged by horses and whipped. He walked away from being stoned also and from being thrown into arenas with wild animals. The animals would not attack or harm him and thereby deny the attempt of the leadership to kill him.

The final straw however was one day they tried to kill John by placing him in a large vat of boiling oil. Something that would definitely almost immediately kill any man normally. John was no ordinary and common man though anymore. He was a Christ infused superhuman creation that could not be killed. Just as you are!

So when they stuck him in the oil he continued to preach the gospel of Christ to all who could hear and was not even touched by the oil at all. This of course freaked out all who witnessed it and freaked out the Roman officials so bad that John became sentenced to isolation on the Isle of Patmos where he wrote his incredibly prophetic and powerful book of Revelation.

This is of course one of the most prolific stories of supernatural intervention where someone cannot be killed ever recorded. This is something that should be as famous if not more so, as the story of Daniel and the lions den. What he knew was what Paul knew and what Jesus taught and lived out. Life was the new agreement, covenant and access point of man and God Almighty. Christ the person is Life and swallowed up creation into Himself and these men and so many more knew this and walked in it as we are to do.

Another man who walked this out was the disciple named Stephen. You might be surprised by that one and I totally understand why. Yet hear me out. In my opinion he was one who also knew that he could not have his life taken from him but could only lay it down and so he did. In Acts 7 is the story of Stephen being stoned. Although to me that is not the story at all. It is the story of Stephen being transfigured and not seeing death.

Why so is because in the previous chapter we see that Stephen is actually transfigured before his encounter with those that want to stone him. This is a sure sign that he has been wholly swallowed up in the life of Christ. Anyone who has been this consumed in the life of God cannot be unwillingly killed. We saw this previously with Moses and then with Jesus and Paul.

Then we see that he cries out to the Lord and says that he willingly gives up his life or breath or spirit to the Lord as he transitions on to the invisible realm. This is exactly what Jesus did upon the cross when He said to the Father that he commends His Spirit to Him. Both of these were a willing handing over of their bodies to a death for a divine purpose.

Stephens death was for a greater purpose than usually taught. When Stephen submitted to that death by stoning, his clothes were taken to the feet of Saul. This is a powerful thing to take a look at. What if by so doing this Stephen actually was handing over his mantle to the man Saul so that the calling and anointing that was on Stephen would come upon Saul so that he would step into the calling to become Paul and accomplish all that was destined for him? Thus Stephen was being one who was showing the greatest love possible to lay his life down for another and become a seed sown that day so that it could bear much fruit.

That fruit was the fruit that became the life of Paul and all of the powerful things that he ended up doing. That moment when Saul met the Lord on the road and he was blinded and then sought the Lord from then on may not have ever happened had Stephen not been obedient in his love and life. Yet he was and that anointing and calling was handed over so that the glory that was intended to come to the earth could come and Stephen decided it was worth it to go ahead and transcend for that purpose.

He could have chose to have been the life we saw with Paul but instead became a martyr and seed for the movement of the glorious gospel. He chose to lay down his life for the murderous spirit upon Saul to be overtaken by the life of Christ flowing through him so that Saul could become the love filled life that was Paul wanting to awaken. This to me was the only way that it became a reality. Death that brought forth Life.

Chapter 8

As the modern day Apostle Bill Johnson says, "If death is a part of Gods plan, then why are we supposed to raise the dead?" I mean it just doesn't get any more clear than that. If sickness is recognized now by the majority mainstream christian circles as not a part of Gods plan because we are to heal the sick, then it would seem to be self explanatory that the same thing would go for death and dying not being intended or designed to still exist.

Immortal and eternal life has somehow been left out of the gospel message and that is absolutely wrong and inaccurate. 2 Timothy 1:10 tells us that Jesus ABOLISHED DEATH and brought LIFE and IMMORTALITY to light through the gospel. The gospel, which is Christ, revealed LIFE and IMMORTALITY as part of our inheritance and blueprint. It revealed that now we are a part of life and immortality and not part of death in any way anymore.

The Passion Translation of this verse says "This truth is now being unveiled by the revelation of the anointed Jesus, our life-giver, who has DISMANTLED DEATH, OBLITERATING ALL OF ITS EFFECTS ON OUR LIVES, and has manifested His IMMORTAL LIFE in us by the gospel." This is such a glorious and radical truth we have have have to catch hold of!

For it is the revelation of this generation that will usher in the fullness of the understanding of those who will be born into the earth and never die as part of the normal lifestyle meant for humanity. The generations soon upon us will see it as abnormal for anyone to die as opposed to abnormal for anyone to live eternally and become transfigured light beings.

Jesus severed from us any chain or cord of death that would try to have us bound. Any bondage of death that would try to steal from us eternal life and eternal freedom in our bodies Jesus cut off and demolished. He abolished death! Thats one of the most powerful things that we could ever have become real to us in our minds and hearts.

Romans 8:23 tells us that an important part of our inheritance in the adoption of sonship is the redemption of our bodies. The promise of sonship in Jesus is that our bodies are to be redeemed and overtaken by the life of the Lord. Our bodies are to become fully aware and manifested as redeemed from any curse or touch of death. This means that we are not to just be immortal spirits that stay clothed in decaying or dying bodies that we lay down. No! We are to have the Spirit of the Lord clothe us from the inside out and consume any record of death or decay within our dna that is a false memory written in.

Any memory or record of death within our dna is to be erased by the truth of life and it more abundant and eternal by the glorious spirt of the Lord Jesus. As Paul said in 1 Corinthians 15 we shall not all die but we shall all transform. Also that these perishable and mortal bodies will put on the imperishable and immortal. Then shall it be true for our entire beings that death has been swallowed up in victory and has no more sting with us.

In Romans 8:11 Paul tells us that the spirit of him who raised Jesus from the dead dwells in you, and that he who raised Christ Jesus from the dead will also give life to your mortal body. Verse 13 then adds to that and says that if we live according to the Spirit of

Christ we will put to death the deeds (memories and falsities of death) of the body and will live.

We were once dead in our trespasses and sins but in Christ we were made alive together with Him and now have no tie or marriage to death any longer. We just have to have our minds renewed to that fact to remove the memories and records of death in our bodies and then manifest it. We aren't to just have life but we are to be life and to give life.

In 1 Corinthians 15:45 it says that the first Adam became a living being and that the last Adam (Jesus) became a life giving spirit. Since He is a life giving spirit we are as well. Just as I wrote about in the earlier part of this book, His nature and truth is our nature and truth. Who Jesus is needs to be understood as the description of who we are by His own design and desire.

A life giving spirit is who you are and have always been intended to be from your genesis. When a caterpillar is birthed into the earth, it is never meant to be anything less than a butterfly. That is its dna, its blueprint, and its eternal reality. You are no different in that your blueprint, genesis and eternal reality is to have your body with your spirit and soul without ever having any of them taste unwilling death.

You are not just meant to not die ever again you are meant, as a life giving spirit, to bring life to all of creation. You and I are meant to remove death from all of the cosmos and creation. This is so much more grand than what we are told we are to be in the vast majority of the church and Body. We are the hope of glory to all of creation by means of Christ within us wanting to be breathed out and released upon the face of all things in existence.

Chapter 9

Jesus tells us in Luke 17:21 that the Kingdom of God is within us. Do you think that the Kingdom of God has any death in it? Do you think that the Kingdom of Heaven has any death in it? Absolutely not! Heaven and God are overflowing with continuous and abundant life eternally.

Within us does not mean that it is in a separate realm existing within us apart from our whole being. As in our body not being a part of that encompassing phrase of 'within us'. Our body is absolutely meant as part of that statement. For as we discussed earlier, our literal DNA and blood within us and flowing through our entire physical being is the part that houses the very DNA and life of God.

Thus our body is intricately connected to the eternal life of God that is living within us and housed in our essence and being. Our physical body then is literally flooded with God and all the fullness of life that comes from God. This is an awe inspiring revelation that should cause us to be so humbled and yet empowered in the nature of who we are and the depth of our purpose to all of creation.

In 2 Peter 1:3-4 we read a powerful thing we need to look at in the context of immortal life and divine eternal existence of our body. It says "His divine power has granted to us all things that pertain to LIFE and godliness, through the knowledge of him who called us to his own glory and excellence, by which he has granted to us his precious and very great promises, so that through them you may become partakes of the divine nature, having escaped from the corruption that is in the world because of sinful desire."

Wow! Peter is telling us that we have been granted all things pertaining to life! That means through the knowledge of Jesus Christ and the glory that He has brought us we can know and live out of everything pertaining to life. That means we can flood any wrong thoughts or knowledge about death and decay with knowledge and truth about life instead and become consumed by that instead.

That through His precious promises to us we can escape the corruption in the world that brings death. We can now by means of Christ and His death and resurrection become partakes of the divine nature of godliness and no longer have anything in us connected to corruption, decay or death. Just like Peter told us in 1 Peter 1:23, we have been born anew with imperishable seed. The very seed of the Father who of course is incorruptible and immortal.

The imperishable seed here is not limited to spiritual rebirth only. This is a complete rebirth of the entire entity that we are as spirit,soul, and body. This imperishable seed was the seed of the person Jesus Christ who was also spirit, soul, and body as well. This was the blueprint of the fullness of us as a divine being living as one with our Father as a three part being.

This is why Paul says in 2 Corinthians 5:4 "For while we are still in this tent, we groan, being burdened -not that we would be unclothed, but that we would be further clothed,so that what is mortal may be swallowed up by LIFE." Look at that! We do not have to die, as in be unclothed by the tent of our body, but we can become swallowed up and clothed fully by life so that any mortality can be replaced with immortality.

Peter and Paul are telling us the same thing. They are telling us that we have been born anew as a new creation in Christ that is supposed to not have any association with mortality, corruption, or death any longer. That we are a new creation born from the very seed of God Most High and have been granted the fullness of His promises pertaining to life. Those promises include the defeat of death and having mortality swallowed by immortality and corruption swallowed up by incorruption. Having all of our being becoming as like our Father and as like our Messiah. Just as how Jesus became fully clothed in life and transfigured before His disciples, so are we to be as like. Fully transformed and transfigured by His life within our entire being until we are no longer bound to any association with decay, mortality, corruption, or death.

Chapter 10

2 Corinthians 5:17 is maybe my all time favorite and go to scripture for so many teachings and talks with others about who we are. It says "Therefore, if anyone is in Christ, he is a new creation. The old has passed away; behold, the new has come." The old is totally gone. The old is completely gone. The nature that existed where death had any part is gone. Christ defeated and removed death and any old thing that pertained to death. Christ made us a new being and creation that was not ever known about before.

We aren't even a restored Adam. We are beyond and different from the Adam that we all seem to have ease in believing was never to die. If we can so easily accept that about Adam than the new in Christ should be just as easy or easier to grasp and believe. We are newer and different than what Adam was also according to this verse. We aren't something that was a mistake corrected or a failure remade over again. No. We are a completely new creation that was never on the earth before. So we cant take what was real before becoming this creation and try to apply it to the new creation we are. We cant use the same rules or formulas or ideas and memories of the previous and try to apply them to the new.

Taking those old rules and guidelines and applying them to the new does no good and creates a mixture that ultimately destroys the new creation same as it did the old. The old ways of living and experiencing God and walking out our existence in these bodies is no longer the same. They are no longer the blueprint or format that we are to operate out of when it comes to our understanding the truth of who we are and the truth of our physical nature upon this earth. Our physical nature has now been fully engrafted into the spiritual nature of Christ that was always intended and predestined for us before time began.

There is a whole new reality, idea, intention, and application to this new creation that was manifested and patterned to us in the life of Jesus and especially in what He showed us as the resurrected Christ. This is all centered around life and it more abundant, incorruptible, immortal, and overflowing now in this new existence and creation. This is why Jesus tells us in

John 10:10 'I came that you might have life and it more abundant."

He came precisely for us to now have the true life that He always desired us to have. The abundant life that is never ending and never able to be defeated and that will swallow up any death in us or around us. The abundant life that has no boundaries or restrictions that were applied to the previous nature. You are no longer just a human bound to what the elemental laws and what science of nature says about you.

You are not just trying to survive for as many years as possible and trying to prolong your death as many years as possible. You are not living off bread, water, vitamins, and nutrients from the earth. You are living because you are in Him and He is in you and therefore you are one with Life. You are one with the One who is called and named Life. You live by the breath, word and Spirit of Yahweh. You live as and are the Body of Christ that can never have any association or submission to death ever again. As long as you so choose this and agree to this and believe this. Its your choice to decide it is real and walk it out from this moment forth as you have become aware of it.

Chapter 11

A major part that needs to be understood alongside of the reality of immortality, is the knowledge of divine health. One does not exist without the other. Grasping that you can walk in divine health and wholeness is the gateway to the catching ahold of being immortal in your physical body.

Kind of like being told all of our life that death is a certain and given so are we told that we have to have sickness, disease, pain, aches, and all other kinds of terrible afflictions on our body and mind. We hear it all of our lives. If you are here on the earth then you are going to have to have pains and aches and sick-nesses.

Why? Where did this mentality come from? Not from Jesus that is for sure. Jesus lived and proved and taught the opposite. His disciples walked out, lived, and taught the opposite also. They followed in His footsteps of teaching and living from divine health.

This is an absolute part of the gospel that needs to be taken ahold of by everyone. Don't just grab hold of futuristic teaching and thought patterns of only one day when you die or lay your body down you can be free from aches, pains, sicknesses and diseases. Grab ahold of that now in Christ!

Jesus was the most whole and healed man to ever live and that was why He could tell others that this was the way they could live also. He did not battle against anything that could try to afflict or harm Him. Jesus did not have the "common" cold or flu. There is no cold or flu that was common to Him and neither should it be to you. That needs to leave your mind and not be something you speak over yourself or your family ever again.

He did not worry about making sure that He had his medicine with Him when He traveled. We need to be the same. We need to not be prepared for a surprise sickness or attack on us.

That is not living from the realm of divine health that you have been given in and through Christ. Now don't hear me wrong. If you are walking through something and have peace about medicinal help, then by all means do it and make sure to keep believing and confessing divine health through it all until you don't need the medicine ever again.

He was not concerned at all about being around anyone "contagious" or that could "make Him sick". He did not avoid crowds, gatherings, or large meetings so as not to possibly run into someone who was sick that could make Him sick. That was never once a part of who He was or part of how He thought about things. When He said that He was the resurrection and the life, He knew that. He lived it and showed it by healing all and raising the dead.

There was no sickness or disease or death that concerned Him or scared Him. Jesus would go right to the lepers and the diseased and touch them and heal them and never once became taken with their symptoms in His body. We have to and must get this truth and have it take roots deep within us and bear that same fruit in our lives.

The fruit of life and immortality with healing in the leaves of our words and actions for the nations. With healing in the leaves of our prayers and declarations over the nations and individuals. With the leaves of healing within the words we speak over ourselves and our family. We must manifest the life giving spirits we are. We must manifest being the tree of life that we are through being one with Christ.

Many years ago in my walk with the Lord, He took me to Isaiah 53 verse 4 and 5. They say "Surely He has borne our griefs and carried our sorrows; yet we esteemed Him stricken, smitten by God, and afflicted. But He was pierced for our transgressions; He was crushed for our iniquities; upon Him was the chastisement that brought us peace, and with His wounds we are healed." Hallelujah by His wounds we are healed! We are healed! Are healed as in past tense. It's already done. Not going to happen or need to happen but is done.

The day that the Lord took me to this passage that I had heard and seen so many times, something new clicked in me. This moment changed my life forever. I knew that in that moment I was being shown that I either was going to believe those verses and live it out everyday or I was choosing that this was not true. That shook me. I knew instantly that I must agree with these verses and never agree again with anything less than.

This meant that I now had to change my whole mind-set around daily life and what was going to be considered common or not with me and my family. I had to revisit the idea of how life looked based around these verses being true. My language had to change as well. I could no longer say anything contradictory to this. I had to leave behind any false beliefs that wasn't in alignment with the fact that by His stripes I am healed right now and forever.

Many people will use these verses and numerous others to pray and stand for health in their bodies when they are feeling bothered or sick with something. Yet won't live from the perspective and mindset of those same verses being true in the sense where they never have to deal with being sick or in pain ever. Its the same faith and the same power that heals that can keep you healed and eternally healed. Think about that. If one is possible then the other is possible.

So from that day on I started to frame differently the way I spoke over myself and my family and the way I believed for my health and the health of my family. I started to declare everyday over myself and my family that health and wholeness was our part and portion. That we were healed and would stay healed and never have any sickness or disease.

If pain would come from somewhere like say a headache, we commanded it to go and said that they did not happen with us. If we would have a stomach ache or unease, we would command it to go and declare it had no part in us because we were healed. They always fled and could not stay.

In the start of living this way it was foreign and odd to us because it was as if we were lying if we were dealing with a headache and spoke over ourself and said that we didn't. Although, we knew as a spirit being that we were actually declaring the truth over a fact and changing the fact with a greater truth. It didn't take long before we were seeing those things not become a part of our lives anymore and seeing our children and ourselves walk in such health that doesn't seem possible to many. Our children walk and live in divine health and my wife and I do as well. We know that it is the normal life for those who believe in what the Lord says is true and when we believe in what He has accomplished for us.

It became something so common and natural for us now that we didn't have to keep making sure to confess or speak out a certain thing all the time. We had transformed our minds which changed out language and changed the manifestation within our body. We had rewritten the cellular makeup of our dna and wrote new neuron paths in our brain that said we were not sickly people having to try to stay alive. We have become life to give life.This is for you also!

Now there have been some times where we have had to take a stand against some things and reject any false things trying to come against us as we have walked in this. Although, the amount of times is super rare and we never lose against those things as we stand firm. We are like many and are growing and learning in this and being perfected in it as time goes on.

As the confidence in that truth grew within me and I saw it manifest as absolution in my life, that was when I felt the desire and the need and confidence to then reach out to pray for others to see them healed.

There was a domino effect for growing in the new mindset of health and wholeness. You start to desire to see it happen for everyone else also.

I fully believe this was what was the pattern for Jesus. I believe that Jesus read about who He was in the prophets and knew who He was as a spirit. As well as then became filled with Holy Spirit within His entire being that consumed His existence with life and godliness.

Therefore Jesus walked it out individually and then was able to reach out to others when the time came to do so for their freedom too. He was the most healed and whole because He knew that was who He was and was supposed to be. He was living from the truth of who He was eternally and not tormented by anything in the temporary. This is for anyone who can believe it.

Chapter 12

So if you can catch hold of the fact that you are able to walk in divine health, then the idea of immortality becomes possible. Because you see that your body doesn't have to and isn't supposed to suffer with anything that would bring death. You become consumed with life. The life of the person of Christ by means of being flooded with Holy Spirit and the same power that raised Christ from the dead.

We discussed in a previous chapter that the Bible tells us that the same power that raised Christ from the dead dwells within you if you are in Christ and that that same spirit and power will quicken your mortal body. Quicken means to "cause to live, make alive, restore to life, or give increase of life." That means that this verse is saying that the same spirit that raised Christ is in you to cause your body to be restored and increased with life until you are made fully alive!

This is so much more powerful than just a good verse to say when we want to get excited about something we have no grid for or to speak over ourselves to try to encourage ourselves when we feel sick and in pain. No! This is meant for us to know the truth about the relationship with our body to our spirit in Christ. We are not meant to have a conflict between our bodies and who we are as spirits . The spirit isn't meant to be the only thing about us that is perfected and whole.

1 Thessalonians 5:23 says "Now may the God of peace Himself sanctify you completely, and may your whole spirit and soul and body be kept blameless at the coming of our Lord Jesus Christ." See in this verse how it is meant for all of the parts of who you are to be in perfection and sanctified wholly. There is none of the makeup of who you are that is meant to be kept in a lesser place than the other.

Also in 3 John 1:2 "Beloved, I pray that all may go well with you and that you may be in good health, as it goes well with your soul." In this verse we see that the health of the soul and the prosperity of the soul is the hinge point for how your body is doing. This is very critical due to the fact that the soul is the mind. It is the part of you attached to the physical engagement with the world and of the natural realm.

Therefore as your mind, or soul, begins to prosper in correct thoughts and the health intended for it your body will by design come alongside also and manifest that same health and prosperity. In other words, as you begin to renew your mind to divine health, divine wholeness, and restoration of life within your body, then your body begins to operate in it and take on that same prosperity of whole health.

This then fully opens the door and the understanding of immortality. For if your body is meant to have nothing cause it to perish or decay, then you are meant to have it eternally. You are meant to have it be so filled and overtaken with life that death has no place with you. You could only lay your life down willingly and never unwillingly.

This is the gospel truth and message that Jesus taught and lived out for all to see and follow in. Since He was the blueprint of the new creation man that was intended for all humanity to be, which He was, this is the map of our existence we are to walk in and walk out.

When Jesus told the disciples to heal the sick and to raise the dead, He wasn't just saying this because it would be really cool and shocking to all who saw it and hear about it. It was showing the disciples and all who would follow in His steps later that there was a defiance against death that we needed to have and a stance for life that we need to have. It was proving that sickness, disease, pain, decay, and death are to have no part in the life of one who is in Christ. Heaven has no place for it and so we aren't to either as we manifest the kingdom of heaven here on earth. We are meant to be life and give life through our entire being and makeup; spirit, soul, and body.

Chapter 13

I have presented to you the evidence and the scriptures and the words. I have expressed my opinion on the matter and have shown you the reasons for why I do. I desire to see everyone else also understand that we are meant for immortal life. If after reading it all you are not convinced or still disagree, you are more than empowered to choose so. There is nothing written in this book that is trying to establish a new gospel message or pathway to a name for myself.

This book is to simply try to reach out and proclaim a message that has burned in my heart for over a decade now and has encouraged me and driven me to live with this focus and the excitement of its truth. I have seen it be a message that was not being taught or touched on by basically anyone at all when I felt the Lord was sharing it with me, to becoming a much more accepted and understood truth within the Body of Christ over the last decade.

I also wrote this book because I feel as if it is a life calling for me to do so and that I had to. I don't mean this in a negative way. I mean it in a humbling and sincere way. I mean that it was something that was wrote in my heart and DNA before I was born and awakened to it many years ago and told my wife that it was going to become a major focal point and revelation of the Body that would bring a glorious shift for all of the earth and creation. All creation and mankind will be impacted by this message as it is part of the amazing gospel and revealing of Jesus Christ.

My humble assessment is that the gospel is incomplete without the inclusion of immortal life being expressed in it. Jesus was adamant about it, lived it and taught on it. Paul was living it and wrote about it many times. Jesus had intention to come to the earth and to defeat death so that we would be able to live and have life. Jesus was revealing the heart of the Father toward man that we should never die but exist eternally with Him as spirit, soul, and body.

I will leave you with these words from the book of Wisdom that can be found in the New Jerusalem Bible.

Wisdom 1:13

"For God did not make Death, He takes no pleasure in destroying the living."

Wisdom 2:23

"For God created human beings to be immortal, He made them as an image of His own nature."

Made in the USA
Las Vegas, NV
13 September 2022

55218131R00049